What's Left is the Singing

Poems by
Mary Kay Rummel

Blue Light Press ◆ 1st World Publishing

San Francisco ◆ Fairfield ◆ Delhi

WHAT'S LEFT IS THE SINGING

1ST WORLD LIBRARY
106 South Court Street
Fairfield, Iowa 52556
www.1stworldpublishing.com

BLUE LIGHT PRESS
1563 45th Avenue
San Francisco, California, 94122

BOOK AND COVER DESIGN
Melanie Gendron
www.melaniegendron.com

COVER ART
"Let go, be still: The Blue Heron"
Colleen McCallion

AUTHOR PHOTO
Steven Wewerka

FIRST EDITION

LCCN: 2010930193

ISBN: 9781421891507

Thank you to those who helped make this book possible:

Colleen McCallion, an artist living in Laguna Beach California. for the stunning cover painting, "Let go, be still: The Blue Heron" oil on linen;

Steven Wewerka for the author photo;

Diane Frank of Blue Light Press whose workshop inspired so many of the poems in this manuscript and to all of the members of the Blue Light Press Workshop;

Patricia Barone, Roseann Lloyd and Maia for their close reading of the manuscript;

to everyone who has given support and feedback on these poems as well as opportunities to publish and read especially:

Ellen Reich, Jill Breckenridge, David Oliveira, Phil Taggart, Marsha de la O, Jackson Wheeler, Britt Fleming and Northography, Jerry Pitkin, Mari Barrone, and Bertha Rogers;

the writers of Onionskin Sharon Chmielarz, Kate Dayton, Carol Masters, Patricia Barone, Nancy Raeburn, Martha Meek, and Cary Waterman;

Gwen Perun whose beautiful music has accompanied my reading of many of these poems, and to the staff at Vermont Studio Center and Art Workshops in Guatemala where some of these poems were written.

Thanks always to Conrad, Tim and Miranda, Andrew and Ann for your inspiration and support.

Publication Acknowledgments

Thank you to all the editors who have published this work, sometimes in earlier versions.

ArLiJo (Gival Press): "Dreaming That Shaman the Tongue," "Blue Windows," "Blessing"
Askew: "This is My Body," "How She Left the Order" (Patterns of Obedience)
Bloomsbury Review: "Adjacent Neighborhood"
Dust and Fire: "Blue Webs" (2009 Diane Glancy Award)
Minneapolis Institute of Art/Northography web page: "Egret"
Nimrod: "Parakeet," "The Heart in its Cage of Bone," "Red Bird in Winter"
Persimmon Tree: "Names for Green" (2010 contest winner)
Rock & Sling: "What's Left is the Singing"
St. Paul Almanac: "Memento"
San Diego City Works Press—Lavanderia: "Giving It All Away"
Tattoo Highway: "Shaking Hands With the Devil"
Turtle Quarterly: "What the Turtle Knows," "Rock From Skye"
Whistling Shade: "Sick in Time of War"
Winterhawk Press—Zeus Seduces the Wicked Stepmother in the Saloon of the Gingerbread House: "Island Ólagón"

"Annunciations" is reprinted as "The Returning" with permission of Bright Hill Press, publisher of Mary Kay Rummel's *Love in the End.*

An earlier version of "Adjacent Neighborhood" appeared in *ArtLife* which is on permanent display at the Los Angeles County Museum of Art.

Early versions of several of these poems were posted on the Northography web site.

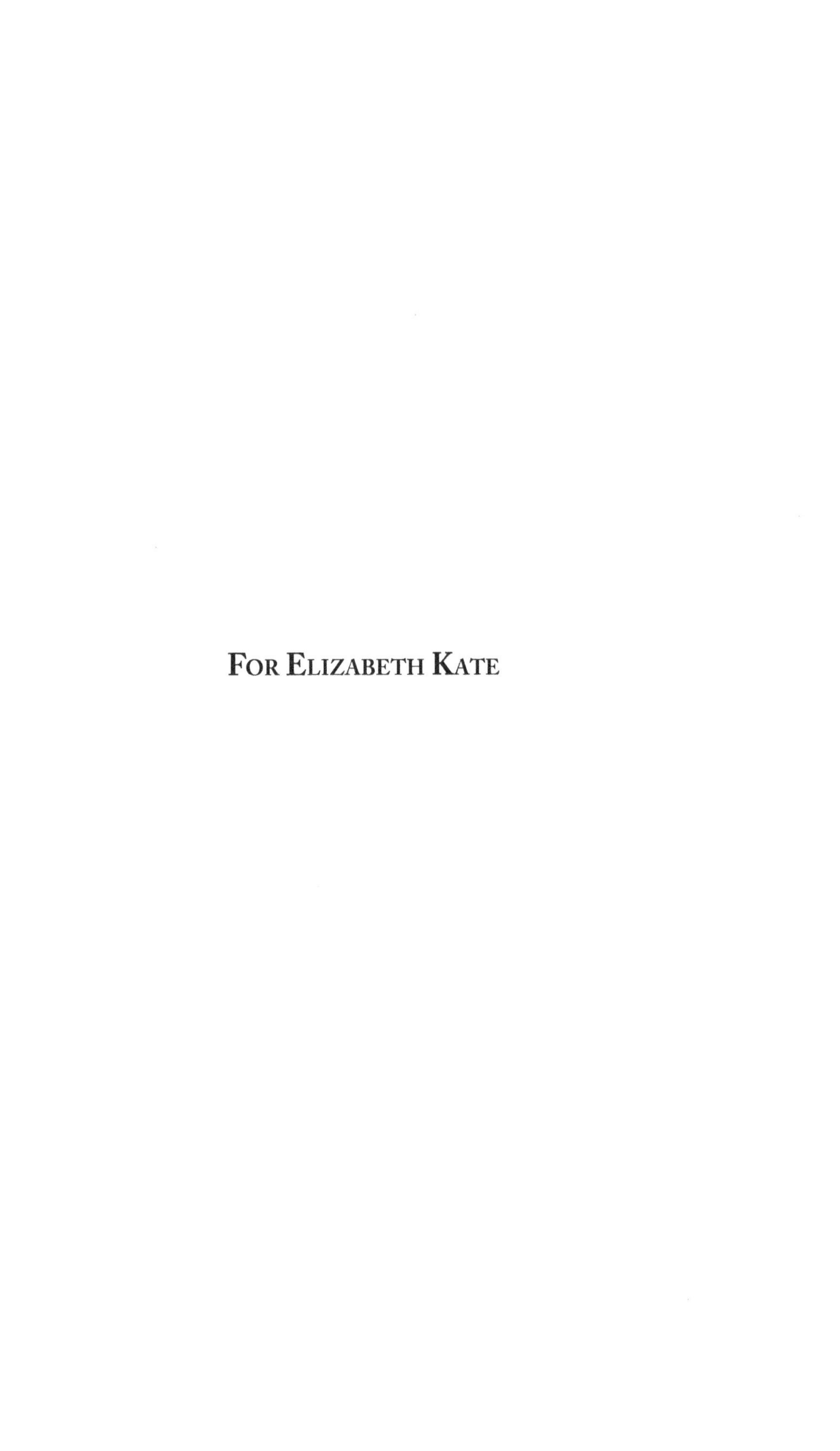

For Elizabeth Kate

Table of Contents

Ear-Shaped Atrium

The Book of Breathing

Last Boat Out

Ear Shaped Atrium

We also lived in two idioms,
in the cramped jargon of the commonplace...,
and in the language of a great dream.

"From Memory" —Adam Zagajewski

Red Bird in Winter

If we say it we grow
feathers or disappear,
so we try not to say
a name, a belief, a death.
We write and paint,
searching, not wanting.
We disappear into details,
heavy frost hushes the grass,
leaves click like fingers,
one word waits
the way the cardinal waits
on the edge of the oak.
The bird, pertinacious, sits,
fat bellied but still,
while trees renounce their leaves.
Every street becomes
the humped back of river's
rage at what comes next,
love, its negligence laid bare.
We wait to be what we will be,
the dim stirrings of one word
a cardinal perched
on the edge of the soul.

The Heart in Its Cage of Bone

A winter wind blasts from the Mississippi
past caves and oil tanks, over train tracks
then down West Seventh where it batters
the girl who walks with ice-crusted scarf
bruising her mouth. Beneath a uniform skirt,
leggings her mother makes her wear.
These she removes and carefully hides
in the bushes behind the bowling alley.

She passes the bar then Nedved's florist.
Ahead, Schmidt's brewery sign flashes
a staccato that stays in her striding bones,
always cold, wrapped in layers, hiding bones.
Her mind churns with voices. Her mother warns:
Stay away from the river; it's dangerous for girls.

Get in the car and help me find Highland Park,
the man says. Voices of nuns push her feet
as she runs from him, *stay pure stay pure,*
runs with guilt in her frightened, Irish bones.

She runs through the stacks of the library.
From the tall clerestory window where the sun
is always going down, she reads the ice
encased river snaking southward.
The dwindling light, spare, unforgiving, is her own.
Frozen there, the chinks in her heart stuffed
with feathers, she imagines a Fra Angelico lazuli,
feels eternity in her bones.

Her thin shoulders hunch, where once were,
and maybe some day will be, wings.

This is My Body

I studied the creek at the place
where it plunges over falls, my face
under water broken and broken again.

When I was a girl I left
my face, my body to find another.
I looked in the church's room of saints.

My body took its cues from these women
with crooked spines, closed eyes,
until I curved and bent my back
under a willow wand neck, the bones
cracking in a leftward lean.

In religion class Father Feeney spoke,
white mane halo around his ruddy face,
his fat fingers shaping air.
Girls, you are growing like this.
His hands forming an hourglass,
his mouth a moue of distaste.

You must stay pure as the holy mother,
pure as the host at Mass,
pure as the Hic est corpus meum
that I say over the bread at Mass.

You have thoughts, words to confess.
You must tell everything.
Confession will save you, he said.

I imagined his heavy flesh under the black,
and looked down my green uniform
at the parts I must keep pure

but his words could not reach me there.
What did he know about my body?
Hic est corpus meum.

My own words could save me.
My body was a tongue
with the sweet host upon it.
My body was a stalk,
lily of the valley growing
beside a wooden house,

baby brothers in my arms,
blushing hearts-ease in a pot of clay
beside the shabby door.

My toes in grass,
my fingers turning pages.

My body sang to wood,
to wheels, to weeds
in the empty lot across the street,

to the boys playing Robin Hood
outside my bedroom window—
my face all angles, my body

a glazier's knife whistling on glass,
anticipation, rain on my lips.

Memento

The day before I entered the convent
I wandered the state fair with my boyfriend
in a jagged dream where
bleachers, stands erupted at angles
from steaming concrete streets crowded
with teens nuzzling each other.
Those who were going to college,
those who worked at the phone company
pretzled together on the roller coaster.

I didn't understand what freedom was
or how easy it could be given away.
If I had understood then
I would have eaten
two more corn dogs,
spent more time circling
on the carousel,
and on that small boat
through Ye Olde Mill,
given more quick kisses
in the tunnel murk.

I wanted to not be ordinary,
already beyond the familiar,
my heart left and leaving.
I went forth the way loons swim
underwater like arrows, slowly arcing
toward what I thought was freedom.

That night my friend gave me a crucifix
wrapped in a silver bow. He held
it outward, until his arms made
an angled cross in the August heat.
The next day I carefully placed it
on a small dorm bed
surrounded by bleached curtains,
an unlikely memento on my pillow.
This I thought was happiness.
This I thought was love.

Abbey Bells

The bus exhaust and noise of West Seventh
will be with her when she walks up the steps.
Just before the doors open, she will turn
to see her mother's stricken face,
her father's shuttered eyes.

She will walk the same circle of oak trees
for five years after that, her life measured
by the brass bell hanging in the cloister
and by golden bells that teachers rang.

She will rise at five, throw on
black layers, run to the freezing chapel.
She will stumble, always last,
up the aisle, collapse in her pew
as the bell rings and her sisters stand
in unison, voices joining
the lift and rise of chant.

At every meal in the refectory
she will finish last.
Two hundred eyes in mute faces
will watch her final bite
as the bell rings
and the nuns stand to pray.

She will walk into liminal quiet
though it takes a long time,
silence as God. She will live alone
with other nuns, not speaking,
scrubbing steps, studying
scriptures, trying to pray.

She thinks God is playing
hide and seek,
that what her heart desires
is always just ahead.
Will he appear if she keeps
following the bells?

Years later after visiting an abbey,
she dreams of that convent,
her tiny room, climbing

floor to floor looking for her name
on a wooden door, but all the names
belong to other women.

She carries her small bundle of clothes,
feeling more lost each sepia minute.
What happens if God stays hidden?
What if the cloister bell rings for prayer
and she turns away?

Hearing comes first and often leaves last.
In between, desire batters the great silence,
destroys itself and returns as one thin chime
in that ear-shaped atrium of the heart.

Confessions

Her Story:

She wanted to be glamorous like women
in the pictures she found hidden among
the church bulletins in her grandparents' porch.
Balancing on one leg on the rounded edges
of the tub, she gazed at her torso wrapped
with a towel, thin as an egret's neck.
She thought the thrill of looking was a sin
but was too embarrassed to confess it,
the guilt growing in her.

She prayed for forgiveness, fasted, promised
to be a nun, rode her bike to church each
hot summer day, afraid that her soul was
getting blacker with the secret, longing
for grown up glamour turned tenebrous
as old potatoes, guilt, the tubers growing.

One Saturday she finally told the priest
asking, *was the sin mortal, do you think?*
Did I give my full consent?
wanting the young priest to tell her
that she was pure as the virgin
on the side altar, eyes upward, head tilted,
veiled body pure, but he stammered,
quickly gave the blessing that forgave
and she flew home released
with images of clean snow,
fluttering behind her belly,
thinking she'd confess it all,
her sins, to him, forgiven.

His Story:

When I started to love her I remembered
the strangled confessions poured out in gloom.
I, sitting in that box, was only a few years older
but she didn't know I was afraid, how the hand
I raised in forgiveness was more for myself.
Bless me, Father, she said. I was too young
to be a father and it was love that beat its wings
in that airless box, fed by the voice brushing
my skin through the screen and the stories
whispered in wounded shadow.

When I told her religious life was the only
cure for guilt I was thinking of my own.
Inside the safe walls of the convent parlor
I finally faced her, told her how my boundaries
had shifted, she had become the still
waters where I found myself.

The black robe revealed nothing of her body.
In my mind she gleamed—an egret whiteness
as if river water had just been poured over her
naked skin and she was drying in the sunlight.
Too late I saw the blessing I had given her was mortal.
A whole church, full of priests, was shaping her soft soul.

Van Cliburn in the Convent

She thought that if she vowed chastity
God would be closer
but one night she sat on the wooden floor,
that she had buffed, shined,
her back straight against the cenacle wall
and listened to the young Van Cliburn
play Tchaikovsky's Concerto in B.
She closed her eyes, imagined his fingers
brushing the smooth keys, then felt
his fingers playing her skin.

Inside she heard a wind-aroused river.
You'd have never known it, looking at her
layered in black serge, breast and hair
covered in white linen, wracked by wanting
in the silence that lives beyond music.
The ceiling of the room rose high and white,
her job to dust its fluted corners and tall
windows, velvet draped against the winter.

Outside the cloister, Randolph Avenue
ran downhill to the Mississippi.
She'd come from the bottom of that hill,
had found the river cave with the granite
the boys called Frankenstein's bed.
She danced to Elvis and Jerry Lee
but didn't know this other music.

The last movement crashed
and turned in her.
Moon became night heron,
floes cracked on the river.
Love opened and opened.

That next Saturday night her sisters
lined the long, unlit hallway to chant
and beat their thighs with small chains.
Instead of penance, she dreamed
Van Cliburn. His melodies grew
through walls around her,
becoming her own body song.

Not Tree, Not Beast

Io, a river goddess, changed into a cow
by Jupiter and tormented by Juno, swam the
Ionian sea to escape.

December that first convent year
gray masonic halls and rooms mirrored
the cutlery sky, no hearth, no rugs
to capture warmth.

Advent music, dirge-like, lauded
a wafer sun, a distant silver monstrance.
Christmas eve midnight, waves
of chant arced and curled.

Vowels swooped and swallowed
as black-clad shadows filled the Spanish chapel,
an incandescence of bells, chant and belief.
At dawn the older sisters woke us with song.

Dream wanderers wove the song lines
warmed the air with old carols,
created heat, washed us in radiance.
Our spirits, ignited, glowed in the dark.

Sweet voices, treble, contralto, coaxed
the sun back to the house of women.
Their voices called out to God
then echoed in the distance.

I was young and heard a different melody
in each ear: the way Daphne, twisted
into a laurel tree, felt sunlight rouse
her topmost branches, the way Io,

changed to a white cow, heard waves thunder
beneath the cliff and knew she would
jump into that sea.

Beneath the Light

La Antigua, Guatemala

Once I knew where to find God.
Sit in the wooden pew,
feel the paths in the wood
beneath my hands and watch
the little house on the altar,
the red light signaling he was in.

A god small enough to fit there,
large enough to save the world
and me in it.

At eighteen I wrote:
In the early morning light
I will dress myself in white
To give myself to you
Who gave yourself for me. . .
A cold love we had then,
locked in, safe.

But here in La Iglesia de San Francisco
the Mayan Mary shines—a shepherdess
wearing lavender to frame her dark skin.
Her veil drapes over the arm
that holds a shepherd's crook.
She reaches for her sheep.

This church cannot hold her
as it couldn't hold us younger nuns.
She is the Lady of Light inside,
and outside this church
her color is jacaranda
sweeping the indigo sky.

I have seen her kneel
on the ground to flatten tortillas,
or roast tomates on the fire.
I have seen her kneel
on dirt and kiss the earth
the way we nuns kissed the floor
as punishment.

It's no trial to honor the spirits.
She breaks from the somber
churches of my childhood
where I knelt hoping to see
her smile, her heart-breaking,
prolonged, deep violet light.

Making the Stations, the Nuns Called It

1

In the nuns' cemetery I pass
a row of fourteen marble crosses,
each with a metal plaque
to mark the times Jesus failed
on his way to crucifixion.

2

We walked from the playground
blasted by brightness
into the shadowed atrium
then further in, stopping at the statues
to pray, going the way we thought
Jesus went, that way we learned
early to look at suffering,
the bereft, a mother, a lover,
a friend, seeing how Jesus fell
three times beneath the weight of it
then kept going the way
the plain chanting empties and fills.

3

Making the stations, the nuns
called it but all those statues
camouflage the emptiness.

an archeology
a bisection
a compendium of our lives

Making the place where we stand
and being there I call it.
I believe in the stations

the warp
the wreck
beneath them

But do they have to mean suffering?
Can't they be a calendar,
that marks us?

a ritual
a requirement
all we know of truth.

4

Last night over the river
the dipper scooped black air,
pointing implacably north.
I am the artist making stations,
marking these moments
of men and women all
going to die
and stopping along the way.

Our Bodies, This Wheeling

1

Three wheels, twelve spokes
nuns buried with their feet
circling an oak, an ash, a cross
like those Irish fairy circles
curses on the one who plows.
Circles within spirals, paths in
ways out, unlike a row of crosses
although the end's the same.
My cousin Catherine's grave is here,
we called her Mother Catherine.
And who was Sister Mary Patrick Tallon?
Her cross says she gave her body to science.
She gave her body and don't we all?

Bear your cross like Jesus
the nuns always said.
Everyone's cross is different,
And the same.

The stations of the cross
could be rooms we live in,
or icons painted to keep
the dying company.

Sex could be a station.
Often the story of women,
the men leaving or gone.

2

He was always gone or leaving.
I love you, he said long ago.
When I am dying it will mean
most to me that you were my friend.
Like Lot's wife I watched him leave
in the long line of those who have gone,
then searched, thinking something
would tell me why he left.
Turned to salt in the middle of my life,
silence meeting the emptiness inside,
some call it a desert, scourge and vinegar.
It was all about his face on my soul.

The Oak

for Geneice

Your white curtained bed stood sentinel
next to mine in the convent dormitory.
We weren't supposed to talk but you motioned
through curtains, pointed to the attic
where we sat on black trunks, stiff
in our new black dresses topped by white collars.
There, surrounded by veils of drying black stockings
we told our young lives. Yours, a soliloquy onstage
beneath a coruscating moon; my world bounded,
bare as enclosed convent cells.

How one life opens into another, then stops.
What if you had not told a friend to call me
after your cancer spread?
I'd think you were still living in L.A.
healing the sick, finding the needed herb.

The day of your funeral I stood in an Irish wood,
touched one of the few oaks left by the English
and thought of you, not knowing you had died.
I heard your theater director voice.

The same moment the nuns were praying
at your funeral, I remembered how your hands
shaped air as you told me of Irish shamans
who touched an oak to travel between worlds.
I think you are one of them, you said.
Stop trying to outrun yourself.

When I was eighteen, you tried to push me
beyond myself, told me that we knew each other
in another life, were priestesses in Greece.
I believed everything you said.
Years later I understood.

When I touched the oak I closed my eyes
the way you said the old ones did and saw
a spiral growing from bleached roots, opening, opening.
I knew that I was circling upward on that spiral.
I knew you were there.

One life bleeds into another, then stops.
That boundary marked by trees and rain-shot air.

Parakeet

The great green greasy Limpopo river
all set about with fever trees. (Kipling)

Music—African Jamaican—furrows humid air,
children chase each other, a parrot swivels
its head, squawks greet the docking boat.

On the ride upriver we watch orange
crowned iguanas, bright ribbons of parakeets
just like those birds I sold as a teenager
in the dime store in downtown St. Paul,
that chattered behind my counter
of seed boxes and small mirrors.

Each time I cleaned the cages one lime green bird
would escape, swoop like a bat through the store,
skim counters stacked with cosmetics,
following its joyful heart.

I climbed after it with a butterfly net,
and daydreamed myself away from there.

Later I walked into the store a nun,
only my face and hands uncovered.
The manager I'd dated
glanced then looked away.

Invisible, I stopped to visit the parakeets.
My fingers, folded deep in wide serge sleeves,
remembered those tiny heart beats and I still
wanted to fly.

Deeper in the rainforest
toucans flash fire above us,
herons guard the shore.
Tiny, wooden houses sleep in the heat,
while a sloth dangles from a palm branch.

Water slaps the sides of the boat,
insistent as memory,
more precise and more admonishing.

Patterns of Obedience

1

Obedience is the most important vow.
Just follow our guidance and you will be holy,

they said before they cut her mind
into rough edged chunks, reordering them
until she became someone who could bow to say,
as you will,
who could kneel and ask permission
to speak, to read,
who would fill out a pattern not her own

like the muskrat, swimming
her one driven trail across black water
as if it were something solid, all day dragging
brown ribbons of weeds from her mouth,
lidless eyes focusing straight ahead,
ahead being all there is, the pond already
freezing at the edges.

Patterns of obedience,
beads on a rosary, cold mathematics
of life lived behind a snow scrim,
held by ice the way it grabs at tires,
clings to gloves, surrounds a soul.

Kneeling, she held up books asking to read
Kristin Lavransdatter, Anna Karenina, L'Etranger.
Each time the Superior, who hated fiction, placed
the book on her own desk, denying permission.

One afternoon a cold wind rustled the cover,
opened a page before her eyes.
Words whispered in that wind telling her
to go forth and read, to never ask again.

2

Snow flecked her black shawl
as she ran to the college library
into the basement literature stacks.

Through low windows
a slow rise of ground to the cloister.
Under a vaulted ceiling of protective oaks,
at first she just peeked at books,
then read, stopping only to copy quotes,
and let words furrow her mind.
Each book, each quote led her
away from the life she was living.

That night a salmon moon
leapt over the tonsured trees,
a rise and fall lamp
in a cracked ice ceiling.

The Book of Breathing

I believe the surfaces of things
can barely hold in what is under them.

"Still Life" —Eavan Boland

As If

The sky is black with cut-glass beakers
of stars. Everything on the mountainside
is crystal—blades of dried grass,
mouse holes, squirrel nests, pine needles.
With abandon the Milky Way spills out
across the night, so sudden so clear.
As if nothing could ever break,
as if no life could shatter.

Aubade

For Conrad

It seems the sea has left you here on this beach of a bed
like the seal that climbs ashore and leaves

the seal pup, the way your mother left you,
born on sand, reclaimed by sea. You still

look young, folded in the dunes, sheets
softening your hard body.

You, sea left, sea called
your face smoothed empty.

I toss all night, wake you to hold me, steal
your covers, leave you now to the sea's churning, recumbent

voice. Found, lost, found again our lives
on this tide bed catch and hold.

Rune

I thought it was a bird
but it was probably a woman
carved by another woman,
buried in a crimson dawn,
left for me to find beside the trail
as I climbed the mountain.

I was looking for what love left
not knowing what's left of love—
in the valley where the wood lily
sometimes danced flamenco—
often was invisible.

I thought it was a bird
but it was probably a woman
defined by what was missing
like the Greek Kore whose hands,
now empty, held gifts for Athena.

We still see them, name them
apple, lamp, sun-dressed stone
as if there were no ruining.

I was looking for what was left,
what was hidden, and I found a rune
for this time marked by loss,
a woman whose rough feet
hurt to touch, whose breasts
were palm shaped, a smudge
now, the color of dried blood.

That night the dead I loved returned
to tell me why they had to die.
Please understand my mother said,
but I could not. Why would you want
to leave these mornings that rise
red from river and mountain, from slate roofs,
on voices of children walking to school?

But we are the fire beneath, she said.
We move the dark around.

I was left then with a flaming wood lily
surrounded by green and in my hand
a rune that was nothing or everything.

Blue Window

At the bar by the eastern window
we toast the eclipse and watch
the moon, smudged entry,
delft cobalt emergence.

All the way home anemone fringe
of surf tingles our skin with sea mist.
Moon attaches a liquid glance
to the tenuous—
frond released from the palm,
clamshell tossed back by waves,
the two of us—
graceful throwaways
sweetened to creamy marigold.

In bed our fingers touch across the sheet.
Eyes change color,
fire collects in our throats.
Moon's sleeve of light spills over rocks
breaks in water and pools in our eyes.
We could be any couple,
our hands, faces held in mercy.

We never wanted to be mundane
but isn't beauty ordinary
and everything else strange?
We wanted the gods to brush our skin.

I still long for you the way
the pine outside my window
once waited for me to touch
its lowest branch.
If beauty escapes and leaves only a sign,
your wrist will wear the mark
of my fingers in the morning.

In the Breath of a Buffalo

The Grand Canyon of the Yellowstone

We skied the canyon ridge
guarded by saw toothed edge of jack pine.
My skis fit inside my husband's tracks
but he skimmed ahead to find a waterfall.

On the gray ribbon of trail, Tim followed his father
escaping the sound of my voice.
Andy struggled by my side.
I'm tired, he whined, *I want to go back.*
Sit on this snow bank, I said, *I'll get your brother.*

I raced down the trail, hearing beneath
the crunch of shuddering snow, an echo
of other skis following mine
into the umber edge of night.

Rushing back with Tim I found
Andy, his eyes riveted to the eyes
of a buffalo cow across the path.
Frozen breath swathed both their heads.

As if crows had flown from behind my spine
I gathered my son, crying, *Mine Mine!*
The great beast moved her unblinking gaze
to me, shook her mangy head and plodded away.

Our three pairs of eyes followed her retreating
flank as she moved away to the right,
to that waiting place of the life unchosen, unlived.

Her tracks, deeper than my arm,
ended in a perfect hoof.
I put my bare hand in, touched the bottom
of her print, energy surging
through me to Andy's cold fingers.

His face shone for a moment as if
he was one of the angels who are all fire,
reminding me how *the child in the womb*
wears many forms—fin, wing, tail,
before being painted for his entrance
with his mother's blood.

Bound to my son
in a kiva of lightning
inside the track of a buffalo,
I understood how *wings once grew*
from the scapula.

The Returning

He sits beside me facing the sea,
young evangelist looking like a crow in his suit.
He follows me on the boardwalk,
I just want to tell you that god loves you.
What? Do I look so needy? Go away,
I want to say, but I once wanted to be holy.

Now my children follow
their own aureoles,
going where belief will take them.
They walked off the way fishermen
in the gospel stories turned,
leaving nets on the beach.

I am going, each announced.
I tried not giving advice.
I tried waking early to write.
Watching them grow I grew stronger,
small and watchful as a lighthouse.
Their courage overcame my fear.

These days I'm letting the sea do my praying,
knowing it doesn't love me.

I love the sea in its thundering concentration,
not like the seal that slides in like oil,

but like grown children who
love a parent as separate
but still part of themselves,
the same way someone sent off
comes back to be with you,

the way last night's full moon,
vaulting over mountains,
filled the Pacific with billions of stars.

Dancing at My Son's Wedding

When Tim and Miranda married, her family didn't dance
until Egyptian music filled the hall and the bride
led her dark haired sisters
whose sinuous arms and hands made cymbals,
whose hips moved to strings, feet to flutes.

Then the uncles called us to join them—
our midwestern bodies fed on rock and roll,
used to Elvis at the grocery store,
the bass line thumping, grinding,
honkey tonk piano moves,
ivory river full of swampy delta blues.

Our bodies stretched into the vibrato
of ancient-new music,
linked us on a wet Cambridge night
with all that sings in desert.

At the church, deep voices in supplication,
a Coptic and Arabic pleading
made us glad to hear the chant,
glad they believed for us.

The dancing called forth my own belief
in sacred things and flesh—
chocolate truffles and purple irises
lutes and lyres, gypsy songs
my sons, their wives, the enchanted little girl
dancing around a white rose in the middle of the floor.

We danced the call and the answer
before the faces of our histories,
caught up in the tangled strings
of a desert violin when the rainy season
is ended and the feast begins.

Catch and Release

For Mari

Northern pike are slimy to touch
two feet of movement,
scaled green radiance
seamed in black
like lead in a tiffany glass.

Thin watery prismatics,
wild rainbows
above the islands
or sunlight on oily streets,
a brush of pink.

We cannot iridesce like this.
There is the gold in Mari's hair.
There is the sheen of love
in her father's eyes,
but our bodies do not shimmer.

A northern pike fights the pulling in,
allows a brief encounter
with Mari's curious eyes,
her quick baby-finger probes.
Thrown back, the fish bolts
turning wine-dark in that splash.

We turn the boat toward home,
slice through shadows in the channel,
through reflections of pine and birch,
their scents woven into our air.
The baby held in her father's arms
swims away into fish-filled dreams.

And to what did we release the northern?
Who knows its happiness?

Blue Webs

La Antigua, Guatemala

1

The need in the market surrounds them,
in the middle stall of the middle aisle.
The infant layered as a coffee bean,
  bluish blanket, red fruit
soft folds of red-white, pulp
then crisp white, shell and then
  the bean, the infant,
the center called *oro*.

Only one corner of the child's face
visible as it sucks,
the whole head covered by a red woven cap,
for now, well protected from malevolence
this *pequeño del oro*.

The mother smiles, her few teeth showing,
veins in her breast, a breath of blue web
that breast, her arm
the circle almost closed.

2

If I listen I can hear this mother saying:

See, she's got it now
  finicky one
  she sucks and sucks
  popping like a cork
  from my breast.

There, a sudden jerk
        like the pull of thread
        a dream pulls through her
See, she is mine
        smelling of warm tortillas
        nursing, clenched fists
        suddenly splay
        like the blossom
        of the pomegranate

My breasts drain into her mouth
        I feel her belly swell
        my breasts soften
        to the insides of a ripe mango
        a web of heat between us
See, I slide my nipple
        from her sagging mouth
        thinking to get back to weaving
        my tapetes and huipiles

But she sends me a message
        I . . . am still here . . . don't
        leave . . . me
For now
I can give her what she needs
and I am happy as the milk filled moon.

3

Why was it so hard for me?
My mother's voice traveled down
my baby holding arm.

Poor baby, he's starving.
You should give him formula.
The doctor disapproving,
You're too weak from surgery.
Not enough milk. He needs a bottle.

My mother standing above me:
You can't do it, neither could I.
You're too nervous.

Why was it so hard
with La Leche at the door?

I'm telling you everything is hungry,
inching toward something else.
Who can stand to be separate
from what they love?
When the milk finally came
blossoming through swollen ducts
it was never a gush, never a fountain
but I knew I could do anything.

Beginning with Skin

For Libby

I hold her in ancestral arms:
an ancient Chinese coin
human geometry, heaven's circle
a shoe, a boat in harbor
a light meter counting hopes
a clock, a cipher
a book waiting to be folded
a tongue with the alphabet it cradles
a rattle moving night

only what is and the vessel it's in
a violet yes, in navy blue eyes
Yes, yes I know you

a prayer bead, a whistle
the clicking of keys
a flare path to follow
through star jessamine,
red valerian, sapphire linen,
curled spiral of fiddlehead fern

we make a beehive for the infant
she opens the earth for us
we are a city regaining its language

she is our pool, our well
we listen, gather
her small sounds.

Camouflage on a Country Road

I watch it ripple across concrete
the monarch caterpillar, fringed
with tiny turquoise eyes on its flanks,
driven by the one leaf that speaks
to its hunger, not at the speed,
but in the arms of light.

A white mare noses what's left of clover.
Hair falls over the eyes she raises as I pass.
She greets me without moving her mouth
from the feed in the way of a nursing baby.
Bees clutch what's left of shredded asters.

Hair rings this earth,
means mirror,
tweezers, peering, plucking.
Fuzz on the face.
Why not let it grow,
loving the gift?
Hair ringing the ears,
each spiky blade.

In October let it be auburn
like my mother's hair when young.
Let it blaze red around my face.
In winter it will turn white
like my mother's thick waves
lost to cancer.

The caterpillar morphs into my mother.
There are soft places on earth
where this can happen, roads
where ghosts are allowed to stand.

There are spaces kept for mothers
without hair,

who touch us without hands,
who speak without throats,
a flowering slow and ornate,
who see us without eyes
as we walk on.

Ocarina

Now that the grass shivers with insects
now that the air is a hive of light
now that dragonflies are mad with sex
          in the gardens of wisteria

Isn't it time to name the colors of our life
the way Mayans wove hibiscus,
papaya and jade into cloths,
the way illuminators painted with cinnabar
          and gold leaf so thin it crumbled.

How can we turn away?
The trees are inscribing their calligraphies.
We need to translate them before
          the ink dissolves.

Let us wrap our wounded memories in hydrangea
turned purple from acidic soil.
Say fifty names for green, that foliate face.
Free all the butterflies in the mariposarium.

Let the bodhran of our hearts beat at matins
and at evensong, ocarinas of color.
We are alive, hungry, still in love
          running out of time.

Let's walk west along the slant lit shore,
watch the sea blossom into lavender.
our bodies, one illuminated book of hours
on this earth with hands full and empty.
Our mingled breath holds our vanishing
          so let the monarchs come.

New wings bless the old pathways.
Let us color each other
in the book of breathing,
the ceremony of the opening
of the mouth, of the body,
the ceremony of leafing.

Dreaming that Shaman, the Tongue

1

Because our tongues move us
from one unknowing to the next,
let nothing obscure the mystery
of that thumb-deep vault
my open mouth,
the cave where Eurydice is lost
where Orpheus enters
only the ante-chamber.

2

Let our tongues meet midway
like dragon and damsel flies crossing
star-laced waters, one thimbleful.

3

A man leads a horned cow,
morning, evening, across a square.
Your tongue is that well-served cow
and the man who shepherds him.
Mine is the breeze from the mountain
that licks your sweating skin.

Across the square a white temple
with gold framed arches, open door.
Your mouth is that temple and my tongue
waits to enter, a redbird losing color in captivity.

4

Your tongue whirls in one place
like a Dervish of Damascus
whose red gown tulips
around his spinning knees.
Mine is your chanting enchanter.

5

Tonight I want to take you
the glisten of your mouth
relearned, reloved.
Tonight I want to take
that shaman of your soul
drumming inside my mouth.

That wild clock spinning us
backward: glass to sand,
sand to freshwater pearl and forward
into a universe of whirling.

Grace

1

What's missing remains
in the echo of train clatter and scream
after it passes like a long needle
through the quilted city
into the pleats of brown and azure hills.

What's missing is a color—
those small lanterns of monarchs
hanging from the pepper tree
or the purple throated hummingbirds
sailing north on the backs of geese.

2

A river makes a garden
in the December desert.
At the base of canyons
gold, coral and persimmon.
The ground is crushed porcelain,
our god in the smell of it.
Together we are red warbler, blue oak
an easy amethyst arrival.

3

Arched between the violin and the dove
a fox, twig grey with black face.
Sun, a stain, we begin to bleach
until we are snow shivering.
A face in the morning—
a comfort I had forgotten.

4

Doubt took the shape of the night train
that knows however far it goes
it will be true.

5

Joy leaps when dolphins
return after a long absence.
The train-roar of high tide,
its sluice-rush, the light
a knife-silver glance
off dolphin skin.

Though invisible again,
they camber between us
as we walk away.

Touching Stone

For Betsy

We trudge through dusk and eager mud
to touch each monolith at Avebury,
some shaped like doors, some
nothing more than blackened teeth
leaning in earth's wet mouth.

A beech tree bleeds into scarlet.
Your pack is a black hump balanced
on your determined back.
In the soggy air a rippling light
envelopes you.

History is more than museum cases
more than sandstone hewn cathedrals
that soar in these undulant low lying hills.
History is not just the sword of centuries,
or jewels in the tower cased in glass.

Each time our genes leap
a star explodes above our heads.

Our history on this earth a spilling,
a reflection, moonlight on fish scales,
sarsens and dreams of those who
dragged them here from Wales,
and from the closer Mendip Hills.

Our bodies made of dead stars and the light is ours.

Heron Moon

The heron carries a stone in her beak,
water tears from her wings.
Bird silence becomes a bridge.
The cloister of heat falls away as you climb.

Above the canyon, ghost orchid
moon releases itself from stone
on wings of mottled ice.

Time, an aspen bridge,
a sun flash on a red-tail.
Each passage spirals you higher.
Pores of granite swallow
the pale egg of moon.

Your shadow, a bridge
inside, leading
as you climb bones of wings.

When your hands become feathers
and your feet go no higher, your words
crack cold in your mouth.
Your body is a sarabande to time.

The origami bird flies higher still.
Your breath, her wings,
your heart, her stone.

The Last Boat Out

Time has become linear and simultaneous.
Every edge is an open window. I can't locate myself,
unless I am everywhere.

"Blackberries in the Dream House" —Diane Frank

Sweet Grass Basket

I inherit the dead.
My body's no longer a small basket
woven from sweet grass and sea weed
left on the rocks to be found.
I'm a large basket now
where those who came before me
dropped the maps they carried.

I inherit the dead.
My body follows but never catches up.
My neck hurts with my mother's pain.
My eyes hold my father's confusion,
close with his stubborn defiance.
My hunger, Mary, my grandmother knew.

Once there were islands where pelicans dove,
the moss-hatted rock on the beach now covered.
Oh tide god, great sand scraper, mountain wearer
I am hollowed from cavernous weathering
undercut like those rocks named skull.

I am a basket swollen with voices,
a skein of words unraveling,
words of the lost like ashes I scatter
across the sea where islands sprout
alluvial folds, sweet grass green after rain.

In the West of Ireland I Hear My Grandmothers' Voices

Ballybunion, Ireland

Sometimes in tandem, sometimes circling,
old ones, like destinations or burdens,
follow me from the peat smoked cottage
from the church moldering in ruins.

We know these fields, the women say,
built them from seaweed.
We touched the clamor-tongue sea
at the edge of the shale,
heard its march, the roar
that took our fisher sons.

Their faces crowd, circling beneath
dense clouds. Voices murmur the way I heard
my grandmothers gossip over tea,
loving to talk about anyone but themselves.

What will the neighbors think?
Be careful! What does Mrs. Connolly say?
Hold your peace.

My grandmothers never knew grand cathedrals.
Their churches were hidden in mouse-grey
damp villages, statues of Mary, whose name
they carried, enshrined on altars where
they lit candles, a wavering city of lights,
a phosphorescence they could live by.

I see a woman bent in her backyard
reaching for a mop, a wooden bucket.
Behind me a girl in a burgundy coat
walks the wet fields alone.

She leans forward, her face luminous.
She is dreaming of how she will claim
her country, the church that hates her.

She doesn't need me.
She is the one I came here to find.

Island Ólagón: My Grandmother's Tale

Musha, child, listen to me.
If I could, I'd take you rowing westward.
When we'd pass the Horse's Mouth
my heart would rise from a cloud
born as I was in the Inish.

We'd pull the boat along the island,
between us and Slea Head
nothing but light. Musha, child,
I would show you where the cows once
softly tread the morning shadows
and all day long the fields followed them,
greening, how the dingle traps the downpours,
holds them fast in its deep mud.

I'll tell you, child, your Blasket Island name,
how you hear it in the ólagón of seals,
so loud you'd think the drowned ones crowded
together, their joints cracking in sunlight
on strong shoulders of rock.

The island, shaped like Bridget giving birth,
always home to daughters with your name.
Now only seals remain and if you go there
in the curragh you will hear them call you,
Mara, Mara, Mara through the fog.

In their coats, the deep red of winter sun
the western waters, the color of your hair,
their eyes, brown as the bay in the wake of a storm,
like your eyes, you quiet one, always turning to the West,
where water drums in fog to towering cliffs.

Musha, child, I would take you to that far country.
I am old and a spool turns no faster than my life.

Bridges

For my Mother

"Not tired please one more."
"Just one more," she'd say.

The maid was in the courtyard
hanging up the clothes.
Down came a blackbird
and bit off her nose.

My brothers and I sat with my mother.
She, exhausted by hours
with washing machine and wringer,
gas stove, cracked linoleum,
five unwieldy children.
"Time for just a prayer tonight."

Please," we'd beg, pull her rough fingers,
"please read to us."

Rhymes made us giggle.
We'd pull each others' noses
between our fingers
not knowing maids or courtyards
knowing clothes billowing on lines,
clean sheets rubbing our faces.

We loved the lilting sound
her voice, our magical sibyl in the rain.

"Not tired please one more."
"Just one more," she'd say.

She led us in a circle, *ring around a rosy . . .*
we chanted, *ashes, ashes,* and fell down.
We learned the idioms that yeasted
our stirred-with-Irish English—

how the baby thrown out with the bathwater,
was the last to wash in long-ago tubs;
how a frog swallowed cured sore throats.

"Yeuw!" we'd shout, "More!"
"Just one more," she'd say.
"Tell us *London Bridge falling . . .*"

What did we know of London?
But bridges we made with our arms
stretched sideways like cormorants
holding out wings for warmth.
Made them fall, lacing our fingers.

Bridges do fall.
Mothers fall.
And we make arches.
The frogs are gone.
Babies are grown.

The rhyme has ended and we are
fading to white like a photograph
of a wet bridge someone might cross over
following rusting lilacs
to a small house marooned on a soggy street,
my mother there in the deepest hold,
far below the watermark.

Names for Green

In the beginning roar and bloom
apple-skin of sea.

Through trance-light
in the current of timothy grass,
the long emerald bodies of conifers call.

Beneath the cow-hoof greening
wend of morning,
see what was wrinkled, smooth,
what was withered, strong.

We will become what we are—
part fern, part birch
on a Picasso earth,
a simultaneity of greens.

An onslaught—always one more
hill dotted with lambs, wool tufts
poking though a comforter.

And in between
such wind-noise of naming.

Let me hold you then in sage,
stem and stamen.

We will enter the brief
cloister of cistercian night,
single-note moss like a moon tasting.
All of it light.

Wild Heather on the Burren

County Clare, Ireland

Earth wanted a martyr
who wanted a terrain.
This is the place.

Strewn with rock, thorn,
nothing grows here
but what is cruel.

Spiked thistles,
ravaged cracks, rain
eats through limestone.

Quickening now, wild heather
to the wound, blue red, amazed
and around it a purple flower

they call bloody crane's bill
tenacious as that bird's claws.
The relentless blooms,

drilling their roots
into sediment of oceans lost,
cannot be undone.

When Stone Speaks

1

What began with sea-roar foam-burst,
ended at rock called *Surf Viewing Woman.*
Her neck grew stiff from listening.

She drank salt and it dried in her.
Her feet, her face, her breasts
calcified, became sculpture.
Hard mass goes well with water.

She breathes in crows and gulls.
Her voice becomes gravel, cracking terra cotta,
gull telegraphs, crow hunger—too much of it.

Her voice of marble from her anchor
speaks air-minded bird sense.

Meanwhile raspberry wind
shears the sky, splitting lightning
leaving a necklace of oyster shells
at her wrecked, untamed feet.

2

Now her eyes are always open, mouth
half covered, like the statue above the sea
in Jerez de la Frontera, made to honor
women of the Spanish-Moorish city
who removed their veils and lived.

Her words, prehistoric
feathery lutes   hollow drums
warble of hummingbirds
without throats
just beyond hearing.

Meanwhile the agitated light slips
through fingers into every fold of sky
while she faces down the wind
in its wedding boots.

Rock From Skye

Once the size of a giant egg
the kind that line the walls of Neolithic
passage graves, now a basalt
cave cleaved open, a stairway
climbs its jagged edge,
steps leading into the heart
of untouchable darkness—
black unquizzical logic
needing neither air nor light.

Like my father and my grandfather's
white haired, straight-backed Scottish reticence.
We would sit listening to hushings, glimmerings,
half-heard things, trying to name them.

The bedrock of this peninsula,
basalt and rhyolite under gorse, dung,
pasture, turf, beneath the Black Mountains,
between the slabs, an alizarin icing.

The tide scrapes handfuls from
its underwater stash and tosses them
shoreward along with shells and red kelp,
the dye still used for sweaters once patterned
so mothers would know their drowned sons.

This rock pushed upward in altered form,
buried centuries, worked over,
finally found my hand, a gift from a land where
every field sprouts a stone-age cairn.

So still, so fossil filled you can hear
the crossing of the waters,
my father and his father
and the wars that shaped them.

When I am taken by genetic undertow
of silence, I squeeze this rock as syllables
flood back in thunder and inflorescence,
words longing for warmth, their smoky roll
under my tongue, a taste of crushed heather.

Sick in Time of War

Your lung collapsed—they are trying to re-inflate it.
You are thankful for the gift of two.

You can't write under the muse of sluggishness.
They are trying to re-inflate it; the dreams come
whispering from all parts of the world.

Under the muse of sluggishness,
the way you blow up balloons, dreams
whispering from the world—peace collapsed.

Your friends march, give up, keep vigil.
You give thanks for the gift of two—lucid eyes,
fingers raised in peace, planets over the city.

Saffron butterfly wings, hands in the blackened
streets, balloons filled with smoke,
so much work, so little time to be agnostic.

Streets black with *agnostic smoke*
each day you learn the deep lore of the earth.
So little time for peace, for the foundations.

The deep lore of each day, a bowl full of meaning,
so much work, the way people leave their gifts
for the lost, for the smoke in the cathedral.

If meaning has a shape you are looking for a bowl.
Footprints everywhere, you're staying on this earth.

Shaking Hands With the Devil

(After viewing the documentary)

Rwanda, the silence of the world
is so heavy above you
that the stars
slow their burning and gaze
at the emptiness, the terrible
jungle, the green hills.

There were houses with eviscerated goats
children in white shirts
women, men wrapped in each other
as if the world had drowned in blood.

What is this day that began with ominous singing?
The bread, the milk, the heated pan
the tree branch swinging in wind
the one bird
perched at its crown
when history turns its back,
when all reason turns
to ash in the grazing lands.

No gods, no men come to help
only children with faces of angels
dead on the road
and covered with flies.

The Lost Bells

1.

Bell of the hollow body, tongue
not yet pealing, school bell, bluebells
my heart would be a bell
protecting tender, unloosed effulgence.

Wedding   dirge bells pealing hours
spray the starlings
like fountains from the tower.
Nine tailor bells—one chimes bones,
one welcomes the wanderer home.

2.

Once I believed in bell rich chants.
The voice of the young monk
vowing to live forever within
the tolling of abbey bells.

Beneath Canterbury Cathedral, a silver
hand bell chimes in a the womb of a crypt
where one candle burns on an altar—
a carving of the lady supporting all that weight.

3.

Maybe faith is a green aerialist,
a hummingbird
hovering but unheard.

You know it by disturbance in air,
that flare at the mouth of the wind bell
breaking the rule I once broke every day.

Mother and sisters I confess.
This week I have broken silence
five thousand times
smashed it like a clay bell,

buried it beneath the sea
under a black and clinquant sky.
The voices of a thousand frogs
ring like muffled bells of the soul.

4.

They say the soul is gone now,
buried in the past,
beneath a matted gravel path.
But the soul will not obey,
carousing in the canopy
with capuchin and howler monkeys.
I want to take in the shout of it

filling me the way a bell fills,
brims over and spills.

Surfacing

That summer we wore a path
around the lake as if around
a clock whose hands kept time
and us in its tight loop.

Sundays we took the children
in the boat, with coffee and papers,
looking whole to others,
no one knowing how we talked
in circles, grim, accusing.

We watched maples turn,
and lose every leaf,
crushed and broken underfoot.

When fire had dulled again to dun,
when we had seen
each other's hurts perfected,
magnified like barren boughs reflected
upside-down in water, no birds
except crows kept their black watch.

The clouds massed, muffled us in snow.
Wordless winter nights each wished
the other gone.

We were digital clocks, numbers flicking
into place, tarnished pennies
in the time bank, a room of months.

We were entrenched in battles
at the back of an island.

With spring we knew, despite the thaw
nothing would grow again from us;
no paths cut through cambered flesh
of clover, wild carrot.

We didn't see white cirrus fingers
drift above us. Didn't know how
love returned to change

the shape of the house we'd made,
unraveling the year of our exile.

Without the help of words, words grew,
welled up as wild honeysuckle
turning clockwise,
swaying between us.

Adjacent Neighborhood

Crows cry over their lost kingdom.
Sight flies over everything, returns
to streets filled with children
ants confused by bare feet
lilacs unsheathed.

In the gardens people toil to a future
wearing passports like haloes.

Laughter or slaughter
outside her door.
She has to go there,
go with her need to love and sleep.

Her voice, ink nicked,
her eyebrows, headlines
reporting news of weather
or hard nights
where faith, hope and sanity
belong to talking heads
counting the dead.

She must hide in her house
or step into their story.

Stations of the Moon

1 Dark of the Moon

primeval
the city at night
made in your hive-like
large-hipped image

2 Ash Moon

in the granite bowl
ashes wait for moon rise
they stir beneath a silver beam
then swell to fill
the world's inner room

3 New Moon

at dusk fish rise
etching the water with
quotation marks

4 Half Moon

brim full
not separate but empty

hold me, a pebble
in the creek, flickering

5 Birthing Moon

gibbous moon, pregnant belly
the sea, the gold struck weaving
from your gypsum loom

tonight the goddess of gingham quilts
the child   a girl   quickens   kicks

like a sleeping giant
quivering the mountain

a sudden seeing tunes the bones
floats down this wave
this sweat this flood

6 Full Moon

wild river full of yourself
help me live
in a dream-thrown sky
the way you do—
painting your changes

7 Illuminator Moon

woods made to bloom
by you alone
I dive into icon gold
your masterwork

8 Traveler's Moon

you show me
towers and tarn
the mirror where you preen

9 Catch Moon

ball or brilliance   last boat out
fat fruit of peeled silver
slips inside monuments and flesh
so they shed the burnt skin
of what is lost by day

10 Moon, the Exclamation Point

sliding overhead
following flight
the way a period haunts
a sentence

11 Crescent Moon

lost in the loose leaves
of your weeping, caught
in the yew tree in Yorkshire
so old, its branches
have bent to root themselves again

12 Moon Above Abbey Ruins

don't ask me where I come from
I only know it's far
and I am getting closer

What a Turtle Knows

1

You watched the turtle bury her eggs
close to the wall. Her black shell shivered
through a forest of lawn, her
thumb head disappearing in roots,
then wedge-shaped feet slogged up a hill.
Halfway there she turned, retraced her steps
then in a semi circle came back
looking for someplace her genes could sink into.
Now, in the pond behind the house, each stick
floats a coin sized turtle, an orange under shell.

2

Once you painted to music composed inside
the Hypogeum, temple of goddess
worship deep within the earth of Malta.
You painted with your left hand, eyes closed.
A she turtle emerged from your brush,
heavy, purple with eggs.
So much ease in that female's release.

3

Go to the pond that lives inside you
Run headlong, like deer among trees
golden threads shaking off fur.

Lift off the way the ducks leave
a small blaze in their wake
as they rise, flash, quacking.

Arc away like the monarch,
freed from the spider web,
who leaves an orange rind of light.

Enter the pond inside you, dive
below the surface to carroty stones,
duck feet.

Laugh in surprise to find
ducks and turtles, dark green,
sunning in monarch light.

The Pale Horse

Chalk Hill—Westbury, England

Gallops across the emerald slope
white in morning steam that hides its feet
making it seem to float across the earth.

Wakes what doesn't change
in us, the I within the eye.

Waits for eons in the chalk hill
until stone age Britons dig it free
with a red deer's antler horns.

Descends to the iron age grave
called the Smithy
to be shod at midnight.

People say there's a secret beneath
the hill where a priestess once stood
to ululate the song of the horse.

She was the first to see
the shimmering in ambient magic
on the eastern edge of Salisbury Plain.

The oracle for Epona, horse goddess, spoke
of prayer or death, the distance between souls
as each listened for the single voice.

The moon wanes, the heart leaves.
The woman speaks and keeps her counsel.
The horse runs, forever.

What's Left is the Singing

The first time I walked into that red
gallery, Van Gogh's iris leapt
from the wall. *There,* I thought, *is God.*

A single chant blossoming into polyphony,
one bulb unfolds snakes that writhe
into a music not human.

The keening heart ascends
from choral rhizomes, dirt, armfuls
of water, violet, deep Chartre blue,
and forges a psalter on canvas.

Fleur-de-lis, iridescent blue
of butterfly wings, released
voice beyond festival and praise,
that smoky sound of life rising
through sword-shaped leaves.

The iris leans to the left as if
pushed by insistent wind.
Fierce love burns each bloom
until it vanishes.

Giving It All Away

After "Pushing a sofa up Mount Everest"
by Mary Norbert Korte

1

My mother raised her fist at the backs
of priests. *Come down off that cross*
if you are god.

Like Sisyphus, each day she pushed
her fear up the mountain

then returned to press her belly
against the ironing board.
The heavy boat powered
by her loose-fleshed arm
plied the endless river of shirts
while her words stormed
the walls of the dining room.

Don't give it all away, she told me.
Avoid the couch.

2

Each day I climb the mountain
after her, following the crickets' fade.
In Devon I hiked the coast trail,
stared down cows that blocked
my path, leapt when snakes sprayed
scattershot from nests.

Climbing down those slate cliffs
weightless with vertigo, I knew the goddess
in small things—
pebbles, cracks, scree, lichen—
the way hummingbirds know
depths of the poppy.

I heard her in cicada
tearing the air to flitters
stitching it back again

Her eyes were holes
like my mothers, like mine.

3

Courage can go all at once
like black birds from cottonwoods,
I'm giving everything away.
Paint is running down
my discarded artifacts.
My begging bowl is in pieces
I carried it from the monastery
when I was new to sex and poetry.

What else could I have done?
I left my ragged couch
beside a mountain trail.
The mountain keeps
what I love inside.
Impossibly yellow poppies
make my words their prayer.

Egret

Snowy egret with boisterous feet
fishes in the shallows each sunset.
It doesn't know me but I know
mating plumage is veil-like in the wind,
bright feet on black stilt legs
attract fish, my knowledge unimportant
before this sea, this burnished air,
before the small tenacious bird,
its gold-brushed head attacked by fat gulls.

At age seven I walked into a classroom
seeing a nun for the first time,
she, opposite of egret, clothed more
in black than white, but also focused,
her slightly bent head listening
it seemed to her own music.
That's what I will do, I thought.

The egret is a keyhole
reminding me of Brancusi's "Golden Bird,"
thin as my husband's legs as he runs
past me on the boardwalk heading West.
Come back, come back I want to call
return like the egret to the rookery,
the wild mustard to the mountains,
but he must run the way the egret's
made to fish, the way my mind
elides nun, husband, bird.

Finding Her

1

You who hear our dreams
in all languages
droning, sometimes singing
in the language of bees,
tear me from sleep
save me from your absence.

Beneath the rattle of palm fronds,
like a dialogue between bird and human
a calling forth, an imitation,
we call you, then listen
for the echo of ourselves.

2

The past returns in waves,
hard spray bringing me
back to the cloister.

Long ago I gave up wearing black
but here and now I shamble—
nun shoes on my feet,
long black sleeves.
Soon I will be hiding my hands,
lowering my eyes.
My closet shifts and seems to sink
the way I sometimes do.

3

In Guatemala old women wear
pomegranate and jacaranda.
You whose name I thought I knew
take me to La Fuenta—the market
where women sell sunlight in cloth.
Let me embrace their woven world.

You, who hides like a finch
in a lemon tree,
who swings like an eagle
between the contrails of a plane,
could the birds be you
stretching out syllables in air?
I read the cimmerian you by starlight.

4

You who break through like an apple
smelling of time outside time
as a prayer book smells of thumbs,
bring me to Glastonbury
where healing springs flow
from a well through a lions mouth
into a vulva shaped pool,
where past and present contend,
clamor, become one sun hungry
end of winter vision where I am
not myself but a hot knowing,
my spirit poured into all my senses.

5

Nameless, unseen, discalced—
I hear your pulse
in arteries of animals.
Around the holy well
the shells of snails
will spiral forever.

Let me rise to face the light
the way a blade of grass
crushed by someone's foot
straightens slowly from its bend,
a yogi practicing her upward-facing-hands.

Blessing

When I turn to face the city on the hills
as the pier releases clinging rays of sun,
the shrieks of gulls skimming our heads
are drowned by Hebrew chants
that drift across surf
from the beach wedding.

The blessing meant for the couple
reaches all who hear
even the libertarians who
stopped me on the boardwalk
to ask what I thought was wrong
with our country and filmed my rant.

Stupidity I answered them, but now
standing on the pier and looking back
at the hill city, feeling sliced open
by the plaint of chant that insinuates
itself into all my closed spaces,
I see that I was wrong.

Now I say it is blindness to the fire
at the heart of things,
to the heat that rises from each of us,
outlines us, the way light etches
hills and mountains in space,
long after the sun has vanished.

We don't see the love that circles us
even as the chanting ends,
blessing the fishermen who dangle
lines in their waiting ritual,
their children who push the sun down
with their arms like old wise ones.

Blessing the tiny snowy plovers that race
waves and rejoice in coming through
one more breeding season,
one more brush with extinction.

Blessing the surfers strung like black signal flags
marking their own private world along the point,
as the wedded couple kisses and stars
begin to reel in the dark.

Notes:

Ear Shaped Atrium

The quote is from the poem "From Memory" by Adam Zagajewski from the collection *Without End: New and selected poems* (New York: Farrar, Straus and Giroux, 2002), p. 269.

The Book of Breathing

The quote is from the poem "Still Life" by Eavan Boland from the collection *Domestic Violence* (New York: W.W. Norton and Company, 2007), p. 19.

The Last Boat Out

The quote is from *Blackberries in the Dream House,* a novel by Diane Frank (Fairfield Iowa: 1st World Library, 2003)

In the Breath of a Buffalo – Italicized sections of the last two stanzas were adapted from lines by Jill Breckenridge (*Winter Heart*) and Maia (*Student of Birds*).

Sick in Time of War—Agnostic Smoke is the title of a poem by Eamon Grennan.

Shake Hands With the Devil: The Journey of Romeo Dallaire is a documentary directed by Peter Raymont. Dallaire commanded the United Nations mission to Rwanda during the 1994 state sanctioned genocide of Tutsis by Hutu militias.

When Stone Speaks was inspired by the work of Medbh McGuckian.

The Lost Bells—part 4 was inspired by the work of Maia.

About the Author

Mary Kay Rummel's poems have appeared in numerous literary journals and anthologies. Andrew Motion, poet Laureate of England, chose several of her poems to be exhibited at London/Art. Her work was short listed for the Féile Filíochta International Poetry Competition in Dublin. She has performed her poetry with musicians and dancers and has read her poetry in many venues in the United States, including the Ojai Poetry Festival at Ojai, California and in England and Ireland. A professor emerita from the University of Minnesota, Duluth, she and her husband Conrad divide their time between Fridley, MN and Ventura, CA where they teach at California State University, Channel Islands.

See marykayrummel.com for more information and to contact the author.

Other Books of Poetry by Mary Kay Rummel

Love in the End (Bright Hill Press, 2008) – a chapbook
The Illuminations (Cherry Grove Collections, 2006)
Green Journey Red Bird (Loonfeather Press, 2001)
The Long Journey Into North (Juniper Press, 1998) – a chapbook
This Body She's Entered (a Minnesota Voices Award winner, New Rivers Press, 1989)

Recent Anthologies containing her work:

To Sing Along the Way, an anthology of Minnesota women poets through history, (New Rivers Press)
Poets Across Borders II (Gival Press)
Nimrod Awards Issues (University of Tulsa)
The SHOp (Cork, Ireland)
Lavanderia (San Diego City Works Press)
Double Lives, Reinvention and Those We Leave Behind (Wising Up Press)
St. Paul Almanac
The Wind Blows, The Ice Breaks (Nodin Press)
Views from the Loft (Milkweed Editions)

Printed in the United States of America

www.ingramcontent.com/pod-product-compliance
Lightning Source LLC
Chambersburg PA
CBHW032019090426
42741CB00006B/659

* 9 7 8 1 4 2 1 8 9 1 5 0 7 *